Contents

Introduction

"Legal advocate" is a broad term, but it encompasses the growing field of advocacy that includes many social service areas, such as immigration law, environmental law, prisoner's rights, and sexual harassment law, as well as more traditional advocacy roles in crime-victim advocacy and child advocacy. Professional legal advocates may be employed by nonprofit organizations, state or federal legal offices, and shelters and community centers. Criminal justice attorneys, social services, and community advocacy organizations are all creating career opportunities in the legal advocacy field, and movements for protecting and enhancing civil rights—such as the Black Lives Matter movement, the #MeToo movement, and the defense of DACA Dreamers—are creating more pushback against injustice, and with that, the need for more legal advocates to help victims navigate the judicial system.

Victim advocates have been an integral part of the social services landscape for a number of years, especially in larger urban and suburban areas. In their work with law enforcement or social services organizations, victim advocates are often the first contact with the courts for people whose lives have been touched by assault, domestic violence, or child abuse. A victim advocate may help guide a crime victim through the court system or help to mediate a solution in a sensitive child custody case. He or she may help a woman escape from an abusive home situation and find a safe place to stay, or a victim advocate may be the most constant adult presence in the life of a child in the foster care system.

Now even smaller rural communities are seeing the need for legal advocates in a number of situations.

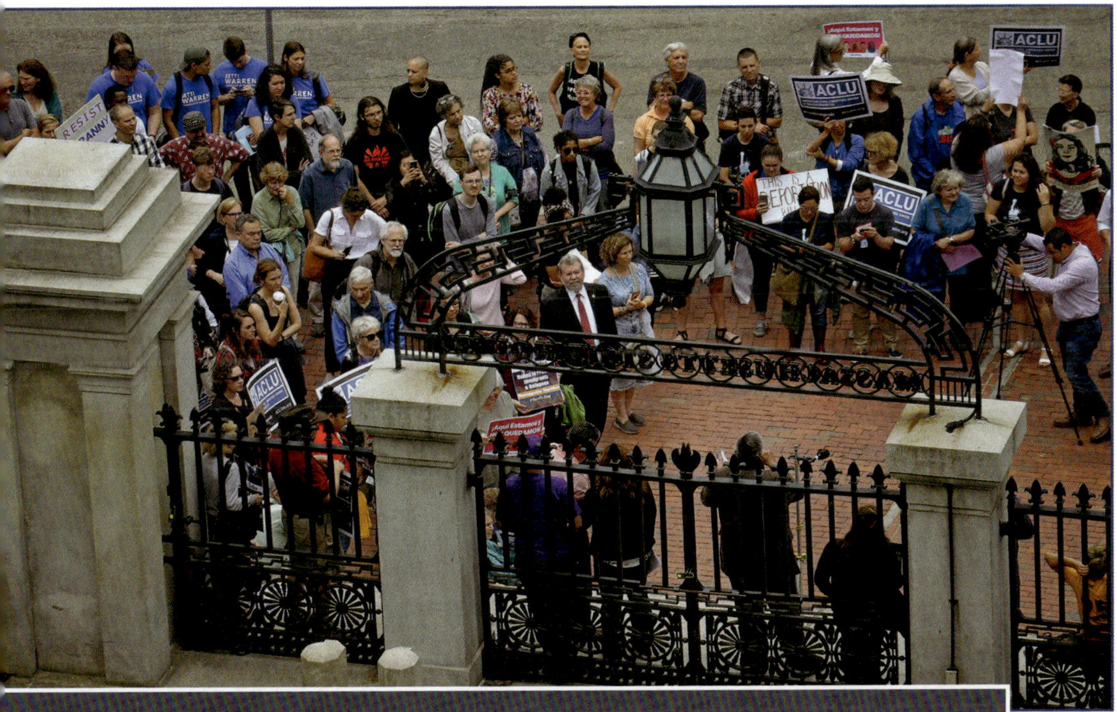

Protestors outside of the Massachusetts State House in 2017 rally against ICE detention requests at the ACLU of Massachusetts Rally for Immigrants' Rights.

Especially in areas with overburdened courts, advocates have become an essential part of a legal team, providing essential research services that allow lawyers to argue cases effectively. For instance, a legal advocate for immigration court may do research for a deportation case in which the individual's life would be endangered by deportation. In such cases, a legal advocate could assemble research for the legal team and provide statistics that support the case for providing sanctuary. In a domestic violence case, an advocate could help the victim navigate all aspects of filing a restraining order and support the victim in court. Or an advocate could go to court on behalf of a Native American tribe fighting for their water rights.

In all these cases, legal advocates provide an understanding ear and an invaluable service to people in need and to the community at large. If there is an area of social justice that interests you, chances are there is a community organization in that area that could use your help as a legal advocate.

CHAPTER *One*

Overview of Legal Advocacy as a Profession

The term "legal advocate" refers to someone who advocates on behalf of others within the legal system. Of course, this definition of advocacy is very broad and could include virtually all aspects of courtroom law and legislation. Many people advocate on behalf of others in the legal system—lawyers, legislators, and even lobbyists. But for the purpose of our discussion, we're talking about the specific position of someone in a legal or social service organization who is authorized to speak on behalf of a person within the legal process. That's the legal advocate.

In most cases, the legal advocate works directly with a person who is navigating the judicial system. That person may be a crime victim, a domestic abuse survivor, a child in the family court system, a prisoner, or an immigrant applying for legal status. Often, the legal advocate is the main point of contact between that person and the court, providing assistance in various ways.

Some of the assistance a legal advocate provides could be informing victims of their rights; offering emotional

Prisoners' rights advocates often work directly with prisoners to help protect them from human rights abuses, including overcrowding, sexual abuse, and mistreatment.

support; accompanying victims to court, mediations, and hearings; or walking them through what to expect as they go through the legal process. They might assist victims with completing paperwork, including applications for victims' compensation, or filing a restraining order. A domestic violence legal advocate could help a victim create a safety plan or help them find a place to stay. An immigration legal advocate might assist the legal team with research, or a prisoner rights advocate might interview prisoners and record complaints about medical care or living conditions. Depending on what field of advocacy interests you, the tasks can vary widely.

There are other legal advocates who specialize in a specific field of policy and legislation. These could include disability advocates, animal rights advocates, or environmental advocates.

Many legal advocates start off as volunteers. This position may be held by someone with some prelaw training or a licensed social worker. In some states, it is possible to become a legal advocate without a degree or certification, but because of the high level of responsibility entailed in the position, an extensive background investigation and drug test is almost always required.

Who Employs Legal Advocates?

Law firms and courts are, of course, the first place you would expect to find employment opportunities for legal advocates. But there are other organizations that employ the services of legal and victim advocates in the course of their business, including government agencies, nonprofits that specialize in advocacy, and human rights organizations. These might include:

- **Police departments.** In some cities and counties, a victim advocate will be assigned to a crime victim as part of the team of first responders.
- **Government agencies.** Some government organizations, such as Medicare, the Department of Education, and the EPA, employ advocates to work on behalf of various issues. If you don't find federal agencies that specialize in your area of interest, check state government agencies, too.
- **Human Rights Organizations.** Amnesty International, the ACLU, the Sierra Club, the

Crime victim advocates also help families of murder victims seek safety and justice. Here, the mother of a victim of a horrific crime consults with her attorney.

Mexican-American Legal Defense Fund, and various other international, national, and local organizations may employ the services of a legal advocate to assist victims of human rights violations.

- **Immigration Courts.** Because immigration is handled by an entirely different system of law than the American judicial system, immigrants are not assigned a lawyer as a matter of course in immigration court and are often in need of adequate representation. Legal advocates are in high demand to help immigrants navigate that system and provide a valuable resource to overburdened legal teams.

BLACK LIVES MATTER

In the wake of the protests in Ferguson and Baltimore, many activists were searching for ways to create more effective and direct legal activism to protect African Americans and end police brutality. Defending the civil rights of protesters was important, but it seemed a more systemic change was needed if justice was going to be served.

Out of this questioning of the status quo, several legal initiatives emerged with the stated goal of transformative change at the policy level with both local and federal legislation.

One such initiative is Law for Black Lives, which describes itself as "a national network of radical lawyers, law students, and legal workers of color committed to building the power of the Black Lives Matter movement." Based in Oakland, Law for Black Lives is thinking big about justice and runs workshops on direct defense of protesters, immigration, and strategies to transform the criminal legal system. They also administer a fellowship for legal innovators, providing financial support and mentorship for "legal innovators seeking to accelerate the impact, scale, reach, and depth of movement lawyering in Black communities."

Another is the activism network of civil rights attorney Ben Crump, who represented the families of Trayvon Martin, Michael Brown, Tamir Rice, and others.

(continued on the next page)

(continued from the previous page)

Ben Crump's new firm will extend this advocacy for social justice causes nationwide, partnering with top lawyers across America to more effectively take on cases all over the United States through affiliated firms.

Their practice includes personal injury, civil rights cases, and wrongful incarceration.

- **Community Advocacy.** Grassroots organizations may also employ legal advocates to work on behalf of specific communities. Tribal advocates may be employed by tribal coalitions or nations, or by private law firms, to work with lawyers defending the rights of Native Americans and sovereign Indian nations. The ADA represents Americans with disabilities, and there are other community advocacy organizations that work on behalf of communities that might experience discrimination or abuse, including African Americans, veterans, and the elderly.

Job Outlook for Legal Advocates

The US Bureau of Labor Statistics (BLS) does not provide salary data for victim advocates or legal advocates. However, legal advocacy falls under the general heading of "social and human service assistants," and according to the BLS, job prospects for those careers are on the rise.

Movements like Black Lives Matter are shining a new light on areas of social justice such as police brutality, civil rights, and wrongful incarceration.

The salary for paid career social service assistants averages about $30,000. The field is expected to grow at a pace that exceeds the average by about 16 percent. An aging population and developments in new areas such as sexual harassment law, immigration law, Native American tribal advocacy, and the Black Lives Matter movement, are expected to impact demand for legal advocates over the next decade.

CHAPTER *Two*

Types of Legal Advocates

Like the legal profession itself, legal advocacy can take many forms. You can advocate on behalf of bills and laws on the legislative level or work as "boots on the ground," advocating on behalf of an individual, accompanying that person to court, or taking his or her testimony. With some crossover, most legal advocacy falls into one of two broad, general categories: victim legal advocacy and public policy legal advocacy.

Legal advocacy is a crucial part of creating safety and justice for victims of crime, children in the foster system, and survivors of domestic violence and sexual assault. These advocates help victims navigate and interact with the legal system and provide resources and support to guide their journey.

Victim Legal Advocates

Victim advocates are among the most long-established categories of legal advocates. Other titles that describe this position include victim service provider, victim coordinator, victim specialist, witness coordinator, or witness specialist.

Legal advocates can help guide and support all kinds of people through the legal system, including victims of crime, foster children, and survivors of domestic violence.

The victim advocate assists victims of crime, including victims of violent crime, victims of assault and rape, and the families of murder victims. The advocate will usually offer the victim emotional support, information, and access to resources they might need, including grief counseling, funeral services, or support groups.

Advocates' roles and responsibilities vary depending on where they work and what their primary duties are. Typically, a victim advocate will work with the victim from the moment he or she is assigned to the case, through any legal proceedings, and beyond. A victim advocate will advise the victim about their legal rights and protections;

provide guidance on the criminal justice process, provide emotional support; help create a safety plan for the victim; assist with paperwork, such as victim compensation applications; and provide referrals for other services the victim might need, including funeral arrangements or even shelter and transportation. As the case goes to trial, the victim advocate may accompany the victim to court. He or she may also help the victim submit comments to courts and parole boards in the criminal case or notify the victim if his or her aggressor is released, or escapes from, prison.

The advocate supports the victim's decision-making, informs him or her of different options available, and helps him or her fill out paperwork. The advocate may contact criminal justice or social service organizations on behalf of the victim, to help get information or assistance. But under no circumstances should the advocate tell the victim what to do. The adovacate's role is to facilitation the victim's decision-making, not to make the decision for the victim.

In addition to working directly with victims, a victim advocate may also staff a crisis hotline, run a support group, or provide counseling one-on-one.

Advocates who work with crime victims must handle extremely sensitive information and are expected to maintain the highest level of confidentiality in their dealings with victims, victims' families, the police, and the public. A victim advocate must respect the confidence of the victim's private information. At the same time, victim advocates are considered "mandated reporters," which means that they are legally compelled to share certain information with officers—for instance, if information is related to their investigation, if a child is being abused, or if the victim is threatening to hurt himself or herself or someone else. It's important to understand the rules surrounding mandatory reporting if you are a victim advocate and to communicate those rules when you begin working with a crime victim.

Child Advocates

A child advocate is a volunteer or social worker, appointed by the family court, who provides assistance to children and families in crisis. The advocate is assigned to a case from beginning to end and is the person who speaks on behalf of a child whose welfare may be endangered by his or her home environment or who has been removed from a home due to abuse or neglect. Child advocates also monitor the well-being of children as they move through the foster care system. Depending on the state, child advocates may be volunteers or salaried social workers.

For both volunteer and professional child advocates, the duties of the position are much the same. Once assigned to a case, the child advocate will be responsible for thoroughly investigating the case and coming up with workable recommendations to improve the child's environment. This could involve interviews with family and friends and consultation with the child's teacher and, in some cases, the child's doctor, to determine the child's welfare. The child advocate will also review records such as medical history, psychiatric history, and academic progress. The advocate may also be asked to observe the child in a social setting to get a better sense of the child's behavior and interactions with others.

Based on these observations and interviews, the advocate will need to keep detailed records for every case

Part of a child advocate's job is to provide counseling for families in crisis. The child advocate may also provide referrals for outside services like food assistance and child care.

they work on, including interview summaries, and make reports of their findings to the court. Formal reports are submitted to the court at least two weeks before court dates, so the judge has time to review the child advocate's case. In some cases, a child advocate may be called to make an appearance in court to discuss the child's welfare with the judge.

Part of the child advocate's job also involves counseling for both the child and their family of origin. It's helpful to be familiar with counseling and therapy techniques, like systems therapy and communication theory. The goal of counseling is to get the family out of crisis, so further intervention won't be necessary. If therapy does not remedy the situation, the child is at risk of being taken away from their family of origin.

If, in the course of their assessment, the child advocate determines that further assistance would be helpful, they can help the family find the support services they need. For instance, the family may be lacking adequate child care or prenatal care or may be in need of food assistance, parenting classes, job training, or substance abuse treatment. The child may be struggling with mental or physical disabilities that haven't been addressed. The child advocate can help the family arrange for the appropriate services and recommend resources.

Domestic Violence Legal Advocates

It's important to distinguish between a domestic violence legal advocate and a domestic violence counselor. A counselor is a mental health professional who specializes in providing support, counseling, and assistance to victims of intimate partner violence. They may also be called a domestic violence advocate or a battered women's counselor, although domestic violence advocates will represent all victims of intimate partner violence, regardless of gender or sexual orientation.

Generally, women's shelters and domestic violence advocacy organizations prefer counselors with a social work or mental health background, ideally a master's degree. Many are licensed or certified social workers, or have graduate degrees in family therapy or psychology. But such a background is not necessary to become a domestic violence legal advocate.

Domestic violence advocates can help victims of intimate partner violence find out about their legal options, and guide them through the court system.

Legal advocates can guide domestic violence survivors through the legal system and help them avail themselves of the legal remedies and protections available to them. These could include protective orders, restraining orders, and child-in-need-of-aid proceedings. Legal advocacy could mean explaining their legal options, helping them to access interpreters, assisting with applications for victim's assistance, and accompanying victims to court. Legal advocates are not attorneys, but they can direct domestic violence survivors toward lawyers and other legal resources.

If they are working in a women's shelter, an advocate might also perform tasks such as intake assessments, and provide referrals for social services, such as food stamps or medical care. They might work at a crisis hotline, accompany a victim to court, or help them find a safe place to live, a new job, and appropriate child care. In all these instances, they are providing support and a sympathetic ear to the victim of intimate partner violence. As with other victim advocates, domestic violence legal advocates should facilitate decision-making, rather than making decisions on behalf of the survivor.

Since they are working closely with women and men who have been traumatized by the people closest to them, domestic violence advocates must be compassionate, nonjudgmental, and sensitive. At the same time, this work can be emotionally draining and stressful. Victims will be dealing with raw emotions and hard truths at a difficult time. It's essential to remain professional while continuing to empathize with a bad situation. It's difficult, but it can be very rewarding. You may be a lifeline for a person getting out of a bad situation.

Immigration Advocacy

With recent changes and proposed changes to US immigration policy, the need for advocates to protect the fundamental human rights of immigrants has never been greater. Immigrants in the United States face a distinct set of problems that are not faced by legal or naturalized citizens. Immigrants who are not legal citizens technically are not protected by the US Constitution, which leaves them vulnerable to indefinite detention, a lack of due process,

Immigrants who face deportation and removal from the United States don't automatically get counsel, so the work of legal advocates may be the only defense they get.

unconstitutional search and seizures, as well as human rights abuses. The entire system of immigration law is separate from constitutional courts, a fact that is poorly understood by people outside the system. To make things worse, immigrant communities may be afraid to report crimes or domestic abuse, for fear of bringing Immigration and Customs Enforcement (ICE) into their communities. Finally, racial profiling that leads to sweeps of legal and illegal immigrants alike is an ongoing problem for immigrant communities.

By working to create policy solutions at the legislative level, supporting legal teams in immigration court, conducting research that supports claims for asylum, and providing strategic advice and legal counsel to support immigration advocacy work, an immigrant advocate can make a big difference in the community and save the lives of immigrants.

There are several areas in which legal advocates can make an impact in immigration policy. One of the main areas is research assistance with asylum cases.

Many people come to the United States in search of protection because they suffer persecution in their home country. If someone is in danger of being harmed in their country of origin because of their race, religion, political affiliation, or sexual orientation, they may seek asylum in the United States to avoid being deported back to a country where they would be in danger.

Asylum is a form of humanitarian protection that is granted to someone fleeing his or her country because he or she is being harmed based on race, sex, religion, sexual orientation, or political affiliation. It's a complicated legal situation, but essential for people emigrating in search of safety. Immigration advocates assist asylum seekers with their claims.

In the current climate, immigration courts are overcrowded, and it's often difficult for asylum seekers to get a fair hearing in the court. Everything that can be done to make a clear, succinct case for asylum in the shortest amount of time is helpful. If a legal advocate can assemble a case that supports a claimant's case for asylum—for instance, gathering statistics and evidence online about violence committed against the claimant's religious group, race, or sexual orientation in their home country—it may mean the difference between life and death for that person.

Another big area of concern for immigrant advocates is removal defense, which involves representing immigrants who face deportation and removal from the United States. Unfortunately, the immigration system does not appoint counsel to immigrants facing deportation. If an immigrant cannot afford a lawyer, they are compelled to argue cases in court against ICE without benefit of counsel. According to a 2016 study by the American Immigration Council, only 37 percent of all immigrants and 14 percent of immigrants in detention have lawyers on their side when they appear in immigration hearings. If they have limited English language proficiency or are unaccompanied children, they are even less likely to have representation—and even more likely to be deported.

Legal representation can make all the difference between being allowed to remain in the United States or being deported and separated from family. Having the benefit of counsel ensures that immigrants can receive a meaningful hearing and could help improve the efficiency of immigration court proceedings, clearing out the backlog of deportation cases.

In addition to representing immigrants in immigration court and defending them from deportation, immigration advocates may also fight for immigrants' rights in other ways, such as securing due process rights for detained immigrants, challenging government regulations, stopping unconstitutional search and seizure, and fighting for the human rights of immigrants in detention centers.

TRIBAL ADVOCACY

Recent events at Standing Rock, which brought the Sioux Nation and oil companies to a standoff over the Dakota Pipeline, shone a spotlight on issues of Native American tribal advocacy and sovereignty in the United States. The status of the Native American nations within the larger context of US law raises unique issues when it comes to the realm of legal advocacy. What is tribal sovereignty, and what does it mean when it comes to legal issues affecting Native American tribes?

Many people think that sovereignty means that Native American tribes are independent nations that can manage their own affairs and create their own laws, determining their own destiny without outside influence. In reality, that's only partially true. Although tribes are able to manage their own internal tribal affairs, their relationship with the US federal government is far more complicated.

Native American tribes are recognized as "domestic dependent nations" that exist within the borders of the United States—meaning that they are essentially dependent wards of the state. Historically, the United States has had a tendency to break treaties, not live up to its treaty obligations, and remove Native American tribes from their original lands, pushing them onto less desirable lands and taking over their resources. You

(continued on the next page)

(continued from the previous page)

can see why legal advocates are needed to fight for tribal rights on many fronts.

There are a number of legal advocacy issues a tribal advocate might engage in.

- **Resource rights.** Indian water rights, fishing, and game rights have been a subject of contention for hundreds of years. Legal advocates are needed to continue to protect resource rights for Native Americans, not only for their priority claims to water use, hunting, and fishing, but also to protect the waterways and land that should be under their sovereign jurisdiction.

- **Gaming Rights.** The development of casinos and legal gaming on tribal lands is a relatively recent development. While there's a widespread misconception that Native American tribes are raking it in with "Indian Casinos," in reality, only a few tribes have been federally recognized, and an even smaller fraction of those are authorized to run legalized gambling.

- **Civil Rights.** Legal advocates can also advocate on behalf of tribal members when they come into conflict with the law, or in other civil rights areas, such as voting rights.

Prisoner Rights Advocacy

Prisoners who are incarcerated in penitentiaries, "supermax" prisons, or similar facilities are often a forgotten population. Since prison is, by definition, not supposed to be a pleasant place to stay, many of the egregious civil rights violations that happen to prisoners—such as overcrowding, sexual abuse, and mistreatment and neglect of prisoner health and safety—may go undetected and unaddressed for years or simply aren't taken seriously. That's where prisoner rights advocates can help.

Prisoner rights advocates are there to make sure a prisoner's basic rights are preserved. These can include medical attention and healthcare, civil rights protections, including the right to freely practice religion, mental health and counseling, and curbing the inappropriate use of solitary confinement, to name just a few. Advocates for prisoners' rights dedicate themselves to helping prison inmates, making sure they retain their constitutional rights and dignity while incarcerated. Prisoner rights advocates may also assist prisoners as they go through the system, helping with preconviction services, presentencing reports, and postconviction remedies.

Overcrowding, sexual abuse, and mistreatment of prisoners pose grave risks to the health and safety of prisoners, and prisoners are often subject to discrimination or abuse based on their race, sex, gender, or disability. Prisoner rights advocacy provides a valuable service by protecting these vulnerable populations.

In many cases, a prisoner rights advocate will be working directly with prisoners, taking testimony,

Some prisoner legal advocates specialize in helping integrate prisoners into society after their release, so they can reenter the workforce and find housing.

investigating conditions in prisons, and interviewing clients. He or she may record and investigate complaints from prisoners about dangerous living conditions, poor medical care, or threats and abuse from other inmates or prison officials. For that reason, you need to be comfortable with the idea of going into prisons and talking to prisoners, sometimes with guards in the room monitoring your conversations.

A prisoner rights advocate may also do research on legal questions pertaining to his or her clients and maintain client files. He or she may obtain information from agencies and institutions related to the case or review records to build a case. Some prisoner legal advocates specialize in issues that released prisoners face when they reenter the workforce and start looking for a place to live.

CHAPTER *Three*

Public Policy Advocacy

Another big aspect of being an advocate is public policy advocacy. Public policy advocates try to effect change at the legislative level, influencing policy on issues that are important to them. Some types of advocacy, such as immigration advocacy, tribal advocacy, and disability advocacy, have a foot in both the victim advocacy and policy advocacy arenas, effecting change on all fronts. Some types of advocacy professions, such as environmental advocacy or animal rights advocacy, fall squarely into the public policy category.

Public policy advocacy involves less individual legal advocacy and more direct political action and coalition building.

Although environmental advocacy is not a common major in universities in the United States, there are some degree-granting programs that focus on activism and community organizing. A good program will cover the history of environmental issues, strategies of political action, and leadership skills. But even if you are not in a degree program, you can develop these skills by

Working as a volunteer and getting signatures on petitions is a great way to get started as a public policy advocate.

working as a community organizer in an environmental advocacy organization. There are also many good books on community organizing that you can use as resources. Coalition building, diversity sensitivity, and grassroots resistance strategies are all skills that could fall into this category.

A big part of community organizing and political action is raising money. This is another skill you can learn on the job as a volunteer, which is how a lot of people get started in public policy advocacy. Grant writing, crowdfunding, door-to-door canvassing, and phone banking are all ways to raise funds for public policy advocacy.

When working as a policy advocate, it's highly likely that you will be interacting with the public. If you are at a public action and a reporter pushes a microphone in your face, you may suddenly find yourself being the public face of your organization. Whether you are fielding questions from the media, leading a meeting, or even updating a Twitter account, it's important to know how to handle public speaking under pressure and avoid reacting emotionally or saying something inappropriate.

More than some other advocacy positions we've spoken about, the field of public policy advocacy is probably most directly impactful on how laws are made, not just guiding victims of laws through the legal system. For that reason, it's an opportunity to learn how the legislative process works and at what point during that process policy initiatives are open to public comment.

Environmental Advocacy

Environmental advocates work to defend the environment by creating public policy initiatives on behalf of the public or the natural world. For example, an environmental advocate could work to protect a community from groundwater contamination by fracking or protect the wolves in a public park from poaching. In most cases, environmental advocates work for a group that advocates on behalf of a single public policy issue, but some organizations (such as the Sierra Club or Greenpeace) advocate on a number of environmental issues and have teams specialized in specific issues under that wider banner.

Public policy advocates often interact with the state legislature through lobbying efforts, organized protests, and legislative testimony. Sometimes, the shortest message is the best one!

In general, the environmental advocate's job is to organize and implement changes in public policy. They may do this by lobbying the state legislature, educating the public, or working on the grassroots level to raise funds. Sometimes a distinction is made between advocates (those who speak on behalf of an organization on policy reform) and organizers (leaders who organize grassroots events such as protests and legislative testimony). But organizers are often advocates and vice versa. If you have a strong commitment to environmental policy reform and social justice, environmental advocacy can be a very rewarding career for you.

WOLVES CAN'T REPRESENT THEMSELVES

In the 1920s, wolves were considered nothing more than a nuisance, and the government allowed the gray wolf population in Yellowstone Park to be hunted to extinction. Since gray wolves were an apex predator in the park, their absence caused a massive shift in the balance of the Yellowstone ecosystem. It triggered what's known as a "trophic cascade" of events that reshaped even the rivers of the park.

How did that happen? Well, without the gray wolves to keep them in check, elk populations exploded, which led to severe overgrazing of the willow and aspen trees needed by the beavers to build dams. Beavers virtually disappeared, and without their dams in place, massive stream erosion altered the ecosystem of the ponds. Marshy habitat was lost, which, in turn, affected other species of plant and animal life, including rodents, fish, amphibians, insects, and birds. Coyotes became the apex predator, and scavengers, such as ravens and eagles, could no longer feed off of wolf kills.

In 1995, when conservationists introduced the Endangered Species Act, the gray wolves from Canada were brought into Yellowstone, and the impact was dramatic. As the wolf returned, coyote populations dropped off, and antelope and fox populations increased. The beaver colonies grew twelvefold, and fish, insects, and songbirds returned to the streams.

The dramatic changes in the Yellowstone ecosystem are still talked about today. But without the tireless work of environmental advocates, none of it would have been possible.

Animal Rights Advocacy

Animal rights advocates promote the humane treatment of animals and educate the public about animal abuse and neglect. They propose legislation and advocate on behalf of laws that will improve animal welfare. Within the animal welfare movement, there are many specific areas of concern, including overpopulation and animal spaying and neutering, medical testing on animals, endangered species populations, and countless others. Most animal rights advocates focus on one or two areas of activism, and gain in-depth knowledge of their chosen area of advocacy.

Animal rights advocates can specialize in several fields within the movement—working in animal foster care, educating the public, or advocating on behalf of legislation. If you want to be an animal rights legislative specialist, you'll have the opportunity to influence animal rights in a variety of ways.

A legislative specialist might do a variety of things to advocate for animal rights legislation. He or she can monitor the progress of pending legislation and regulations through state and federal law-making processes and draft formal comments and position statements on behalf of the organization. A legislative specialist can strategize

Animal rights advocacy groups often campaign for livestock to be given better living conditions, like getting outdoors and having space to move around.

grassroots and lobbying advocacy efforts, organize press conferences, or attend meetings with community boards and associations. He or she may also be active on the social media front, creating legislative alerts on behalf of the organization; creating informational materials, literature, and displays; and appearing at community events with literature on behalf of the organization. A legislative specialist may even get active in fundraising, organizing a fundraising event, a phone bank, or online fundraising effort.

CHAPTER *Four*

Paths to a Legal Advocacy Career

Qualifications for legal advocacy can vary widely by state, and by what sort of legal advocacy position you are interested in. In the United States, most states have no legal requirement for victim advocacy. But for positions as a career legal advocate, many employers want prospective candidates to have previous experience working with crime or abuse victims in some capacity, or some coursework toward a social work or law degree. There are also many ways to become credentialed as a legal or victim advocate, including certificate programs which offer credentials in programs as short as forty hours.

You should check your state government website or talk to your guidance counselor, to find out what the requirements are for legal advocates in your state. But depending on where you live, you have many options as you choose your path to a career in legal advocacy.

Volunteer Work

In most cases, a legal advocate's first experience in advocacy is as a volunteer. Even with a professional

Coursework toward a law or social work degree can only enhance your career prospects. Here, students do research in the library of Harvard Law School.

credential, many prospective employers will want to see some experience working as an advocate, either in the field you are applying for or in some related advocacy field. Volunteers often work with the courts or in social service organizations. Women's shelters and some police departments will work with volunteers as victim advocates. Working as a volunteer advocate not only looks good on a résumé, but it gives you a good opportunity to test the waters and see if this is the kind of work you would be interested in doing day in and day out, before you commit to a credentialing program.

How to Land the Job

First, do research in the area you want to work in and see which issues resonate with your concerns. For instance, if you know you are interested in animal rights, are you passionate about no-kill shelters? Or are you more interested in protecting endangered species? It's best to pick one or two issues to focus on, at least initially. It's easy to burn out if you focus on too broad a selection of causes.

Next, identify organizations that support your goals and share your ethics. Are you excited about new and creative initiatives in reforming prison law? Or are you really interested in helping protect immigrants from detention or deportation? Look at what organizations in your area are doing and see what kind of work is available that fits your skills.

Finally, call that organization and volunteer. This may seem counterintuitive if you are looking for a paying job, but there is no better way to build experience toward a paying job in advocacy. Any amount of experience is better than no experience, and it's something you can add to your résumé for the next job. Plus, it's also a great way to make contacts and meet people in your chosen field.

As a volunteer, you may feel overwhelmed and unappreciated. You may not understand how making coffee and photocopying fliers is helping to advance your career in any way. But it's important to maintain a good attitude. Show up on time, wear clean and appropriate clothes, and maintain a friendly and willing attitude with everyone you meet. Remember, every day you volunteer, you are making an impression on the people you work

Volunteer work is a great way to learn skills and build your résumé. These volunteers in an Urban Organic Community Garden are learning about sustainable farming initiatives.

with. You should treat it as an opportunity to impress your future employer. If you are enthusiastic about the job, work hard, and listen to instructions, you're bound to make a positive impression on your coworkers. Then, when a paying position opens up in the organization, you will be the very first person in line for the job.

Volunteering also gives you an inside glimpse of the organization and the work they do. Remember, you're checking them out just as much as they are checking you out. And you'll be learning by leaps and bounds every day you work in an actual advocacy organization, even as a volunteer. Learning all you can about the culture of an organization can be an invaluable step on your career path—even if what you learn is that you don't want to work there!

Volunteer work is a great way to build a résumé toward the career you want. You can also work on building skills, advancing any credentials you may need, and of course, writing to your representatives about causes you are passionate about.

Education

Education requirements for legal advocacy will vary widely depending on state. Some legal advocacy organizations prefer students who are working toward a law degree. Other states have strict requirements on credentialing, but many don't. For areas where there is no standard credential requirement, such as victim advocacy, there are organizations that are striving to provide their own nationally accepted credentialing program, such as the National Organization for Victim Assistance. They offer a professional credentialing program for victim advocates. The entry-level credential is a forty-hour training certificate, but there are also longer programs.

For positions that require a lot of legal research and team support, a background that includes experience with legal terminology and resources, such as online legal libraries and research services like LexisNexis, would be helpful. Once you are working with a legal team, some law firms will even pay for your further training and help you develop your career.

Child advocates are important allies for children in the foster care system. In some cases, they may be the most consistent adult in a child's life.

In somc states, victim advocates are required to be licensed social workers. Social work accreditation requirements vary by state, but in many cases it requires a bachelor's or master's degree in social work (BSW or MSW). Depending on what type of advocacy work you are looking for, this may be a requirement for you. Many jobs in victim legal advocacy would prefer at least some coursework toward a social work degree, just to demonstrate that you are familiar with the terms and concepts in use by social workers.

For public policy advocacy, such as environmental law advocacy, preparation in your chosen field could take a different form. A background in natural sciences, for example, would be helpful for an environmental advocate. An environmental advocate for the Chesapeake Bay Foundation would have to become familiar with the migratory birds of the region and would find the answers to such burning questions as, "Do blue crabs hibernate?"

How to Become a Child Advocate

For a paid child advocate position, most organizations will look for someone who has completed at least a bachelor's degree in social work, preferably a licensed social worker. However, they may also look for someone with completed coursework in another social service field, such as psychology, sociology, or early childhood education.

Most states also look for an individual whose work history includes advocating on behalf of, or working with, children or other vulnerable populations. Counseling or therapy experience, teaching experience, or even working in nursing homes or in the field of domestic violence, would all be useful preparation for being a child advocate. Volunteer work as a child advocate would certainly count as previous work history and would be a great way to get started in this profession.

Professional child advocates can make between $30,000 and $50,000 a year, according to the Bureau of Labor Statistics guides for social workers.

How to Become a Domestic Violence Legal Advocate

Depending on the state that you live in, you might need a state license to practice in the field. But there is little consistency among state requirements for domestic violence advocates. According to the NIH, a survey of

In many cases, domestic violence victim advocates start out as volunteers in a women's shelter. Good legal decisions can help keep victims safe.

training requirements for providers in different states yielded wildly variable results. Generally, domestic violence advocates are expected to have a familiarity with accepted theories about domestic violence, including the concept of the cycle of domestic violence and the issues of power and control that tend to manifest in violent relationships. Before taking on a role as a legal advocate, you will probably be required to do up to forty hours of training on dealing with domestic violence victims.

Talk to your local domestic violence advocacy group or women's shelter to find out what you can do to become a legal advocate. Often, the first step toward becoming an activist in this area is volunteering. Check to see what resources and training are available in your state.

BECOMING A CASA VOLUNTEER

The most common path to becoming a volunteer legal advocate in child court is through the National Court Appointed Special Advocate Association (CASA). Together with state and local programs, the CASA program supports and promotes court-appointed volunteer advocacy. CASA volunteers are appointed by judges to advocate on behalf of abused and neglected children. They make sure that children don't get lost in the system or get shuffled into inappropriate group or foster homes. Once assigned to a case, a CASA volunteer stays with each case until it is closed and the child finds placement in a safe, permanent home. For many children in the foster system, the volunteer advocate assigned to their case may be the only constant adult in their lives.

You can contact your local child welfare organization to find out how to train as a CASA volunteer in your area. The CASA website maintains a current list that is searchable by state.

CASA volunteers must be twenty-one years old, be willing to go through background checks and complete the training program, and be willing to commit to the program until your first case is closed.

Once you are approved to enter the program, all CASA volunteers go through a thirty-hour preservice training. The training program covers such necessary topics as courtroom procedures, the juvenile justice system, and social services for children who have been abused and neglected.

When the training program is completed, a judge will appoint the volunteer advocate and assign him or her to a case. CASA volunteers stay with a child until his or her case is closed and the child has been placed. You will need to be available for court appearances as needed, but most cases require only about ten hours a week, according to the CASA site. The average case length is about a year and a half, and most programs require the volunteer to commit to at least one year's service.

How to Become an Immigration Advocate

There are many advocacy organizations that work to defend the fundamental rights of immigrants, including national civil rights organizations. The best way to get into immigration advocacy is to contact your local immigration law or advocacy organization and find out what they need. To actually represent immigrants in court, a law degree and familiarity with immigration law are, of course, essential. But the backlog of immigration cases is at an all-time high, and immigration advocacy lawyers need assistance from legal advocates to support their caseload in court.

Starting as a volunteer can lead to paid positions assisting lawyers in all aspects of immigration law litigation. The Immigrant Legal Resource Center (ILRC) and the National Immigrant Justice Center are two national organizations that are good places to start getting information about immigration advocacy.

How to Become an Animal Rights Advocate

Animal rights advocates can be paid employees of an animal rights organization or volunteers, depending on their level of expertise and experience. Most animal rights advocates start out as volunteers for an animal rights organization, such as the Humane Society, People for the Ethical Treatment of Animals (PETA), or the American Society for the Prevention of Cruelty to Animals (ASPCA). They then grow within those organizations and take on more responsibility, growing into advocacy roles such as educator, legislative specialist, or public relations specialist.

To become an animal rights advocate, you don't need a lot of training or education. Volunteering at an animal shelter or working as a canvasser for an advocacy organization are both great ways to get started.

How to Become a Prisoner Rights Advocate

The requirements for becoming a prisoner rights advocate may vary depending on the state. But in the United States, to become a legal prisoner's advocate it's generally a requirement to have at least a bachelor's degree in law, and a diploma in legal practice. For that reason, many consider this field to be the domain of pro bono lawyers.

However, there are also many things you can do to support prisoners as a volunteer or paid organizer in an advocacy organization. If you're interested in becoming a prisoner rights advocate, a call to a human rights organization such as the American Civil Liberties Union, Amnesty International, or Human Rights Watch, might be a good place to start. The ACLU is active in prisoner rights, prison reform, and civic engagement. Some grassroots organizing organizations for prison reform prefer people who have had experience in the prison system or may even prefer someone who has been incarcerated.

How to Become an Environmental Advocate

The best place to start as an environmental advocate is to do online research on an area of environmental advocacy you are interested in. You will quickly come across the organizations that specialize in your field of interest. If you want to save seals and dolphins along the Pacific coast, for example, the Surfrider Foundation would be a good place to start to learn about public policy initiatives that help protect their habitat. Even some state parks have grassroots advocacy programs to advance policy initiatives through the state legislature.

Background Check and Drug Test

Because of the high level of responsibility in the legal advocate profession, background checks are almost always necessary. In addition to safety requirements, there may also be federal regulations to adhere to, depending on your state and what type of tasks you are responsible for. Contrary to popular belief, a felony conviction will not necessarily prohibit you from working in a government job as a legal advocate. In fact, some advocacy fields—such as prisoner rights advocacy—might actually prefer to hire someone who has experience in the prison system! However, ex-felons may be barred from performing certain job duties, such as working with children, depending on the nature of their felony.

Especially if you are applying at a federal agency or working with children, you can expect a preemployment drug screening for any government or social service job, as well as random drug testing once you are on the job. In some states, failing a preemployment drug screen, or refusing to take one, can disqualify you from future consideration for any type of civil service job in the government. In Michigan, for example, a positive test would result in an applicant's disqualification from civil service for three years.

CHAPTER Five

Working as a Legal Advocate

A day in the life of a legal advocate can vary widely, depending on what type of advocacy work you do. Some advocates, such as those who work in domestic abuse court, spend a lot of time working with victims of domestic abuse, navigating all aspects of filing a restraining order and accompanying victims to court. In other cases, a child services advocate could work closely with small children and spend a lot of time out of the office working as a case worker, performing inspections and interviews. In general, here are some of the things you can expect to do as a legal advocate, working within the court system.

Research and Record Keeping

As part of a legal team, legal advocates spend a lot of time researching and assembling a case on paper. For instance, in a deportation case in which the individual's life could be endangered by deportation (such as in the case of a gay person who could be murdered for their sexual orientation in their home country), a legal advocate could assemble

Legal advocates may work as part of a larger legal team. The team discusses the evidence it has discovered and decides the best way to make a client's case.

evidence about the immigrant's home country. Such evidence could include statistics on how many people have been killed for their sexual orientation in that country or recent news stories about hate crimes in that country. This evidence could be crucial to present to the judge in support of an application for asylum.

Similarly, they may spend a lot of time documenting cases and hearing testimony. A prison legal advocate, for instance, might tour a facility, or a child advocate may spend time in a child's school or interview a teacher. This involves less library time but requires a high degree of organization.

Meticulous research and record keeping is often a big part of a legal advocate's job. For instance, a child advocate will be responsible for keeping detailed records on each child's case. This may include interviews with family, teachers, and doctors; maintaining medical records, academic records, and psychiatric history records; and making regular reports to the court about the child's welfare. An immigration lawyer's legal advocate might spend late nights assembling data about an immigrant's home country in order to support a case for asylum. Someone's life may depend on your ability to keep clear, organized records.

Navigating the Justice System

Navigating the justice system is also a big part of legal advocacy. For instance, an advocate in a domestic violence case might accompany the victim to court, explain the court proceedings, and help the victim file a restraining order.

Sometimes, legal advocates allow speedy resolution of cases outside of court by representing the victim in mediation. In child custody cases, it is often the case that the family will try to resolve issues in mediation, with legal advocates present. This is often seen as a gentler way of resolving family and domestic issues without involving the courts.

Knowledge of the legal system is key. Although on-the-job training and professional credentialing can supply this knowledge, a big part of the legal advocate's job is to help people navigate the "red tape" of the courts. The more you know about what to expect from the legal system and where to get answers, the more useful you will be to the communities you serve. Similarly, it's important to be able to convey that information to the person you're advocating on behalf of in a clear, concise manner. Communication skills—sometimes in more than one language—are necessary.

"I HEARD THE CLANG OF THE STEEL DOORS CLOSE BEHIND ME"

Prisoner advocates do important work to maintain civil rights within the justice system. But it takes a special kind of person to walk into a prison and deal one-on-one with prisoners who may have been convicted of serious crimes. Even people who have nerves of steel can feel intimidated once they actually get inside prison walls.

"I can still recall the first time I was escorted into the bowels of a prison unit to interview a client, and heard the clang of the steel doors close behind me as I walked into prison for the first time," says Sharon Robertson, a prisoner advocate specializing in civil rights.

Robertson and her colleagues at North Carolina Prisoner Legal Services provide a range of legal services to over 37,000 inmates in 78 North Carolina state prisons and more than 250,000 people incarcerated in North Carolina's 98 county jails. She's been using her civil rights expertise as part of the civil rights team for 16 years. But even she gets chills when she recalls her first experience entering a prison on behalf of NCPLS.

When she interviewed for the job at NCPLS, Robertson says, her interviewer asked whether she could handle being alone in a room with a person who had been charged with a serious crime, because sometimes there would not be a guard physically standing in the same room to assure her safety.

"Every person is entitled to be treated with a certain degree of respect. I also make sure not to place myself in any situation that compromises my safety when interviewing the inmate," Roberston adds.

Communication

In many communities, being bilingual is an asset on the job. Particularly in immigration advocacy, it's important to be fluent enough to explain complex legal requirements to people who may not speak English as a first language and translate written documents accurately.

Communication is not just about how you use your words. It's also about what is not said. It's important to be able to remain calm and communicate in a nonconfrontational manner with a variety of people, including representatives of the court. When mediating a resolution to a case, you may find yourself across the table from an aggressive domestic partner or an abusive parent. If you get frustrated easily, or have a problem

When you're working with people who are going through traumatic experiences, empathy and emotional intelligence are crucial.

with authority, you may experience friction as a legal advocate. As the person who's advocating on behalf of a victim in court, this could also impact your client, and it is important that you represent them well. That's why it's important to be able to talk to all kinds of people—not just the people you advocate on behalf of, but also judges, lawyers, clerks, and security personnel. There are many resources online for emotional intelligence, leadership, and communication skills, if these are skills you want to develop.

A Balance of Skills

As you can probably tell from what you've read so far, legal advocacy requires a delicate balance of people skills, analytical skills, communication skills, and research skills. You'll be working with people who may be going through one of the most traumatic experiences of their lives, and you'll be helping them navigate a legal system that is often impersonal and intimidating. For victim advocates, part of your job will be helping victims of crime and abuse cope with stress, shock, and trauma in the wake of their experiences. It's rewarding, but it can also be difficult work.

Since you may be working with people who have been traumatized emotionally and physically, empathy is crucial to the work of a legal advocate. Victims of domestic violence, people who are facing deportation, crime victims, and abused children are among the people you will be dealing with every day. They will be experiencing overwhelming stress that is not only psychological and emotional, but possibly physical and financial. The ability to listen and empathize, without judging or becoming frustrated, is critical for a victim advocate.

CHAPTER *Six*

The Future of Advocacy Work

The long-term outlook in the field of legal advocacy is good. Evolving issues such as sexual harassment law and environmental concerns about fracking and water rights, for instance, are coming to the forefront,

Members of the indigenous community march in Toronto, Canada, in November of 2016, to express solidarity with the Dakota Access Pipeline protesters.

creating demand for professional advocates in new areas. As people become increasingly aware of how political issues affect their communities and the people around them, the demand for professional advocates, particularly organizers and legal assistants, is likely to increase.

HOLLYWOOD AND FARM WORKERS STAND TOGETHER FOR #METOO

When women working in Hollywood began to report their experiences with sexual harassment in the entertainment industry in late 2017, they found an unlikely ally: Latina farm workers.

The Alianza Nacional de Campesinas, an organization that represents the mostly Latina women who harvest the country's fruits and vegetables, published an open letter of solidarity with the actresses. These brave farmworkers understood the feelings of shame, guilt, and helplessness described by the entertainers and let them know they weren't alone. "We believe and stand with you," the letter said.

Together, the workers and the entertainers marched in Los Angeles, building solidarity. The following week, a coalition of Hollywood women, including Shonda Rhimes, Salma Hayek, Gwyneth Paltrow, Rashida Jones,

(continued on the next page)

(continued from the previous page)

Jennifer Lawrence, and Reese Witherspoon, published their own open letter, announcing the creation of a new coalition, #TimesUp, and a legal defense fund to help survivors of sexual harassment and assault.

"To the members of Alianza and farm-worker women across the country, we see you, we thank you, and we acknowledge the heavy weight of our common experience of bring preyed upon, harassed, and exploited by those who abuse their power and threaten our physical and economic security," their announcement read.

However, the nonprofit sector is greatly dependent upon external influences, such as the availability of federal funding, philanthropic donations, and the state of the economy. Recent changes in tax law may create a ripple effect, as large philanthropic donations are taxed at a different rate, discouraging large donations. When budget cuts hit the nonprofit sector, it affects their margins—and often reduces the number of employees and the salaries available.

The field of legal advocacy is ever evolving, and new areas are expanding every day. This resource has covered only a fraction of the possibilities within the legal advocacy field today, and it's difficult to predict with any certainty what trajectory the search for social justice will take in the future. But here are just a few of the nascent areas developing in the area of legal advocacy.

Employment Law and Sexual Harassment

In the wake of the #MeToo movement, a tidal wave of support for victims of sexual harassment in the workplace has swept over the employment law landscape. Human resource departments and several independent organizations—not to mention law offices—are taking sexual harassment policy more seriously than ever before. With that new focus come new opportunities to work for the rights of women in the workplace to be free of harassment, stalking, retaliation, and intimidation.

Transgender Rights

The civil rights of transgender people go far beyond the question of which bathroom to use. Health care discrimination, antitransgender violence, and support for transgender service members and veterans are just some of the issues taken on by transgender legal advocates. For more information on how you can do more to support transgender legal rights, look online for groups and organizations that can offer support.

Gun Control

For years, the National Rifle Association has had a stranglehold on Congress when it comes to gun control legislation. In 2008, none of the presidential candidates even dared to voice support for common sense gun control laws. This is changing fast. In the wake of the

Gun control is a quickly evolving area of public policy advocacy. Here, students march in Los Angeles in the wake of the Parkland shooting.

Parkland shooting, millions of students took to the streets in support of gun regulation. A poll by Quinnipiac University in Colorado found that 66 percent of American voters support stricter gun laws, up 14 percent from 2015. If this is an area of concern for you, you can contact organizations like Everytown for Gun Safety, the Brady Campaign to Prevent Gun Violence, and the Coalition to Stop Gun Violence.

Creating a Positive Change

Careers in advocacy offer a unique opportunity to fight for what you believe in. Standing up for the rights of others can be tiring and frustrating, and there may be times that you feel like you are fighting an uphill battle. But the rewards of helping people and creating positive change on behalf of your ideals are worth it.

Glossary

ASYLUM Protected status that is granted by a nation to a refugee who has fled his or her native country in fear, usually as a result of persecution or violence.

COMMUNITY ORGANIZING A process by which communities come together, led by an organizer or organizers, to create social movements based on their mutual concerns; works by building a base of community members, mobilizing them to act, and developing leadership and relationships from the membership.

CONSERVATION The act of conserving resources, such as water, vegetation, natural ecosystems, or wildlife.

CREDENTIALING The process of acquiring a credential that proves one's fitness for a particular job, such as a diploma, certificate, or other document proving a person's qualifications, or attesting that they have finished a course of training.

DETENTION The act of being detained by the state, or the act of detaining someone in official custody. In relation to immigration, detention is not governed by the US Constitution and can be indefinite.

FELONY A serious crime, defined as punishable by more than one year of prison or death.

GRASSROOTS Describing a political movement that starts from the "ground up," among everyday people, rather than a "top down" initiative.

HABITAT The natural environment or home of an animal, plant, or other type of organism.

INITIATIVE A plan or program that is launched with the intent of solving a specific problem.

LEGISLATION Laws, or a body of law; the process of making laws.

LEGISLATURE The governing body that makes the laws in a country or state.

NONPROFIT A organization that uses all the money in its budget to run and do the work of the organization.

PHILANTHROPIC From the Greek word meaning "love of humanity," describes a person or organization who seeks to promote the welfare of others, usually by donating money to good causes.

POLICY A high level plan outlining the general goals and acceptable procedures used by a government body, which is used to guide present and future decisions.

PROTECTIVE ORDER Also known as a restraining order, an order used by the court, often in a domestic violence case, intended to prevent harassment, stalking, or assault, and to protect a person, business, or other entity.

PROVISIONAL Temporary; serving for the present time, but likely to change or expire.

SEXUAL HARASSMENT Inappropriate harassment in the workplace or other professional situation that involves unwanted sexual attention, inappropriate sexual advances, or obscene remarks.

SOCIAL WORK Work that is dedicated to the betterment of social conditions in the community, for example, by feeding the hungry, improving conditions for the poor, promoting children's welfare, or offering aid to the elderly.

SOVEREIGNTY The full right or power of a governing body to govern itself, without interference from outside governments.

TRAINING Teaching or developing the necessary skills for a particular art, profession, or job.

For More Information

American Civil Liberties Union (ACLU)
125 Broad Street, 18th Floor
New York, NY 10004
(434) 220-5610
Website: https://www.aclu.org
Facebook: @aclu
Twitter: @ACLU
Instagram: @aclu_nationwide
Founded in 1920, the ACLU works with a broad mandate to defend individual rights and liberties as guaranteed by the US Constitution. Some of their areas of concern are human rights, immigrant rights, disability rights, reproductive rights, civil rights, and free speech.

American Society for the Prevention of Cruelty to Animals (ASPCA)
424 East 92nd Street
New York, NY 10128-6804
(212) 876-7700
Website: https://www.aspca.org
Facebook, Twitter, and Instagram: @aspca
One of the oldest animal rights advocacy organizations in the United States, the ASPCA was founded in 1866 with the mission "to provide effective means for the prevention of cruelty to animals throughout the United States."

Brady Campaign to Prevent Gun Violence
840 First Street, NE, Suite 400
Washington, DC 20002
(202) 370-8100
Website: http://www.bradycampaign.org

Twitter: @BradyBuzz
Instagram: @bradybuzz
The Brady Campaign was founded in 1974 as the National Council to Control Handguns (NCCH). It was renamed the Brady Campaign to Prevent Gun Violence after Jim Brady, the Presidential Cabinet member who was permanently disabled by a gunshot during the Ronald Reagan assassination attempt of 1981.

Canadian Civil Liberties Association (CCLA)
90 Eglinton Avenue E
Suite 900
Toronto, ON M4P 2Y3
Canada
(416) 363-0321
Website: https://ccla.org
Facebook and Twitter: @cancivlib
Founded in 1964, the CCLA advocates for civil liberties, human rights, and democratic freedoms of all Canadians, including indigenous populations.

Canadian Resource Centre for Victims of Crime (CRCVC)
100–141 Catherine Street
Ottawa, ON
K2P 1C3
Canada
(613) 233-7614; 1-877-232-2610
Website: https://crcvc.ca
Facebook and Instagra: @crcvc
Twitter: @CRCVC
Since 1993, the Canadian Resource Centre for Victims of Crime (CRCVC) is a nationwide organization providing

support, resources and education to survivors of serious crime in Canada.

Everytown for Gun Safety
450 Lexington Avenue
New York, NY 10022
Website: https://everytown.org
Facebook: @everytownUSA
Twitter: @Everytown
Instagram: @everytown
Led by former mayor of New York City Michael Bloomberg, Everytown for Gun Safety is an American nonprofit organization advocating for gun control and gun safety. Everytown was founded in 2014, when it combined Mayors Against Illegal Guns with Moms Demand Action for Gun Sense in America.

National Association for the Advancement of Colored People (NAACP)
4805 Mt. Hope Drive
Baltimore, MD 21215
(410) 580-5777; (877) NAACP-98
Website: http://www.naacp.org
Facebook and Instagram: @naacp
Twitter: @NAACP
Since 1941, the NAACP has been the premier organization for federal civil rights advocacy on Capitol Hill. The organization was a leading force for enacting the 1964 Civil Rights Act, the 1965 Voting Rights Act, the 1968 Fair Housing Act, and countless other landmarks of civil rights legislation.

National Immigration Law Center (NILC)
3450 Wilshire Boulevard, #108–62
Los Angeles, CA 90010
(213) 639-3900
Website: https://www.nilc.org
Established in 1979, NILC is one of the leading organizations in America dedicated to defending and advancing the rights of low income immigrants. They are engaged in impact litigation, policy advocacy, and training, and they work closely with other civil rights organizations.

National Women's Law Center
11 Dupont Circle NW, #800
Washington, DC 20036
(202) 588-5180
Website: https://nwlc.org
Facebook and Twitter: @nwlc
Instagram: @nationalwomenslawcenter
The National Women's Law Center was founded in 1972, when secretaries at a public interest law firm made four demands: better pay, more women attorneys on staff, work on women's rights, and no more serving coffee.

Sierra Club
2101 Webster Street, Suite 1300
Oakland, CA 94612
(415) 977-5500
Website: https://www.sierraclub.org
Facebook and Instagram: @sierraclub
Twitter: @SierraClub

Founded in 1892, the Sierra Club is the nation's largest and most influential grassroots environmental organization and works to promote renewable energy solutions, ensure a clean, safe water supply, and protect endangered wilderness areas.

Surfrider Foundation
PO Box 6010
San Clemente, CA 92674-6010
(949) 492-8170
Website: https://www.surfrider.org
Facebook and Instagram: @surfrider
Twitter: @Surfrider
Based on the Pacific coast of California, the Surfrider Foundation is dedicated to protecting the world's oceans and beaches through a worldwide activist network. Exclusively focused on coasts, they fight offshore drilling and plastics pollution and advocate for clean water.

For Further Reading

Alexenko, Natasha Simone. *A Survivors Journey: From Victim to Advocate*. Seattle, WA: Amazon Publishing, 2018.

Alinsky, Saul. *Rules for Radicals.* New York, NY: Random House, 1971.

Blackmon Lowery, Linda. *Turning 15 on the Road to Freedom: My Story of the 1965 Selma Voting Rights March.* New York, NY: Penguin Young Readers, 2015.

Bolles, Richard N. What Color Is Your Parachute? 2018: A Practical Manual for Job-Hunters and Career-Changers. Emeryville, CA: Random House, 2017.

Chang-Muy, Fernando. *Social Work with Immigrants and Refugees, Second Edition: Legal Issues, Clinical Skills, and Advocacy*. New York: Springer, 2015.

Furgang, Kathy. *Getting a Job in the Legal Profession.* New York, NY: Rosen Publishing, 2017.

Garner, Bryan A. *Legal Writing in Plain English, Second Edition: A Text with Exercises*. Chicago: University of Chicago Press, 2013.

Harrigan-Pedersen, Nurys. *Make Your Mark: The Smart Nonprofit Professional's Guide to Career Mapping for Success*. New York, NY: Morgan James Publishing, 2018.

Klein, Rebecca T. *Cool Careers Without College for People Who Love Reading and Research.* New York, NY: Rosen Publishing, 2018.

Kritzer, Herbert Morris. *Legal Advocacy: Lawyers and Nonlawyers at Work.* Ann Arbor, MI: University of Michigan Press, 1998.

Lore, Nicholas. *The Pathfinder: How to Choose or Change Your Career for a Lifetime of Satisfaction and Success.* New York: Touchstone, 2012.

Petrikowski, Nicki. *Working for Tolerance and Social Change Through Service Learning*. New York, NY: Rosen Publishing, 2015.

Prentzas, G. *Careers as a Paralegal and Legal Assistant.* New York, NY: Rosen Publishing, 2014.

Sack, Rebekah. *The Young Adult's Survival Guide to Interviews: Finding the Job and Nailing the Interview*. Ocala, FL: Atlantic Publishing Group, 2016.

Schilling, Vincent. *Native Defenders of the Environment.* Summertown, TN: Seventh Generation Press, 2011.

Singer, Peter. *Ethics in Action: Henry Spira and the Animal Rights Movement.* New York, NY: Rowman & Littlefield, 1999.

Thompson, Laurie Ann. *Be a Changemaker: How to Start Something that Matters.* New York, NY: Simon Pulse/ Beyond Words, 2014.

Wright, Amy Conley, and Kenneth J. Jaffe. *Six Steps to Successful Child Advocacy: Changing the World for Children.* Thousand Oaks, CA: Sage Publications, 2013.

Bibliography

Buckley, Cara. "Powerful Hollywood Women Unveil Anti-Harassment Action Plan." *New York Times*, January 1, 2018. https://www.nytimes.com/2018/01/01/movies/times-up-hollywood-women-sexual-harassment.html.

Bureau of Labor Statistics. "Occupational Outlook Handbook: Social and Human Service Assistants." Department of Labor. Retrieved February 8, 2018. https://www.bls.gov/ooh/community-and-social-service/social-and-human-service-assistants.htm.

CASA (Court Appointed Special Advocates) for Children. "What Does it Mean to Be A CASA Volunteer?" Retrieved February 8, 2018. http://www.casaforchildren.org/site/c.mtJSJ7MPIsE/b.6350721/k.112A/What_Does_It_Mean_To_Be_a_CASA_Volunteer.htm.

Crews, Gordon A. *Critical Examinations of School Violence and Disturbance in K-12 Education*. Hershey, Pennsylvania: Information Science Reference, 2016.

Criminal Justice Degree Schools. "Criminal Justice Careers: Victim Advocate." Retrieved February 8, 2018. https://www.criminaljusticedegreeschools.com/criminal-justice-careers/victims-advocate.

Davis, Howard. *Human Rights and Civil Liberties*, Oxfordshire, UK: Taylor & Francis, 2003.

Day, Elizabeth "#BlackLivesMatter: The Birth of a New Civil Rights Movement." *The Guardian*, July 19, 2015. https://www.theguardian.com/world/2015/jul/19/blacklivesmatter-birth-civil-rights-movement.

Dengler, Charise. "Sharon Robertson, Paralegal. North Carolina Prisoner Legal Services, Linvillle Falls, NC." Law Crossing. Retrieved February 8, 2018. https://www.lawcrossing.com/article/1474/Sharon-Robertson

-Paralegal-North-Carolina-Prisoner-Legal-Services-Inc -Linville-Falls-NC.

Eagly, Ingrid, and, Steven Shafer. "Access to Counsel in Immigration Court." American Immigration Council, September 2016. https://www .americanimmigrationcouncil.org/sites/default/files /research/access_to_counsel_in_immigration_court.pdf.

Immigrant Legal Resource Center. "Asylum." Retrieved February 8, 2018. https://www.ilrc.org/asylum.

National Center for Victims of Crime. "What is a Victim Advocate?" Retrieved February 8, 2018. http:// victimsofcrime.org/help-for-crime-victims/get-help -bulletins-for-crime-victims/what-is-a-victim-advocate-.

National Immigrant Justice Center. "DACA and the Dreamers." Retrieved February 8, 2018. http://www .immigrantjustice.org/issues/daca-and-dreamers.

PETA. "Effective Advocacy: Planning for Success." Retrieved February 8, 2018. https://secure.mediapeta .com/peta/PDF/EffectiveAdvocacyGuide_FINAL300 .pdf.

Reed, Silas. "How to Become a Prisoner Advocate." Law Crossing. Retrieved February 8, 2018. https://www .lawcrossing.com/article/5070/How-to-Become-a -Prisoner-Advocate.

Skalicky, Sue. "Tension Between Police and Standing Rock Protesters Reaches Boiling Point." *New York Times*, October 28, 2016. https://www.nytimes .com/2016/10/29/us/dakota-access-pipeline-protest .html.

Stelloh, Tim, Molly Roecker, Chiara Sottile, and Daniel Medina. "Dakota Pipeline: Protestors Soaked With

Water in Freezing Temperatures." NBC News, November 21, 2016. https://www.nbcnews.com/storyline/dakota-pipeline-protests/dakota-pipeline-protesters-authorities-clash-temperatures-drop-n686581.

Stover, Carla Smith. "Training and Certification for Domestic Violence Service Providers: The Need for a National Standard Curriculum and Training Approach." National Institute of Health. Retrieved February 8, 2018. https://www.ncbi.nlm.nih.gov/pmc/articles/PMC4231530.

University of Iowa. "Definition and Examples of Sexual Misconduct." Retrieved February 8, 2018. https://opsmanual.uiowa.edu/students/sexual-misconduct-datingdomestic-violence-or-stalking-involving-students/definitions-and-1.

Whifte, Ron. "What Kind of Drug Tests are Given for Civil Service Jobs?" Work Chron. Retrieved February 8, 2018. http://work.chron.com/kind-drug-tests-given-civil-service-jobs-23744.html.

Williams, Susan. "An Overview of Indian Water Rights." Legal brief. Retrieved February 8, 2018. http://opensiuc.lib.siu.edu/cgi/viewcontent.cgi?article=1283&context=jcwre.

Index

About the Author

Growing up outside of Washington, DC, as the child of self-described "policy wonks," Janet Harvey has a strong interest in political advocacy and activism. She has worked as a door-to-door canvasser, a grant writer for various nonprofits, a policy writer, and as a legislative correspondent in the US Senate, answering mail for Senator Herbert Kohl (D-WI). She also writes for the National Superintendent's Roundtable, a professional membership organization of engaged school superintendents.

Photo Credits

Cover El Nariz/Shutterstock.com; back cover, p. 3 and interior pages border Piotr Adamowicz/Shutterstock.com cover and interior pages (map) © iStockphoto.com/Pingebat; pp. 5, 22 Boston Globe/Getty Images; p. 8 Stockbyte/Thinkstock; p. 10 Indranil Mukherjee/AFP/Getty Images; p. 13 Daniel Leal-Olivas /AFP/Getty Images; p. 15 Creatista/Shutterstock.com; p. 18 Iakov Filmonov/Shutterstock.com; p. 20 Snezana Ignjatovic/Shutterstock.com; p. 28 Michael Kelley/The Image Bank/Getty Images; p. 31 Hero Images/Getty Images; p. 33 Alexandros Michailidis/Shutterstock.com; p. 36 Rolf E. Staerk /Shutterstock.com; p. 39 Brooks Kraft/Corbis News /Getty Images; p. 41 Yellow Dog Productions/DigitalVision /Getty Images; p. 43 Monkey Business Images/Shutterstock.com; p. 45 SeventyFour/Shutterstock.com; p. 52 fizkes /Shutterstock.com; p. 56 Prostock-studio/Shutterstock.com; p. 58 arindambanerjee/Shutterstock.com; p. 62 Hayk_Shalunts /Shutterstock.com.

Design and Layout: Nicole Russo-Duca; Editor: Bethany Bryan; Photo Researcher: Ellina Litmanovich